Pieced by Donna Perrotta
Applique by Janice Irick
Quilted by Julie Lawson

'4 Seasons' is wonderfully versatile. You'll love this collection of quilt patterns that will entertain you throughout the year.

Celebrate each of the four seasons by trading out the small quilt that you hang in a special place in your home.

Or make a large quilt that celebrates all four seasons. You'll love the unique colors that separate the seasons yet blend together into one stunning quilt.

When making a 'Block of the Month' quilt, I like to finish one season at a time...
Month 1 - Piece the center and border squares,
Month 2 - Applique the design, and
Month 3 - Assemble the quilt.

You'll love every block and every quilt.

Suzanne

MATERIALS FOR EACH MONTH:
We used *E.E. Schenck Company/ Maywood Studio* "Woolies" flannel fabrics.
'Color of the Month'
Summer/Rose Pink - page 4	Fall/Yellow - page 18
Winter/Blue - page 12	Spring/Green - page 24

'Fat Quarter' (18" x 22") each for Piecing:
    White A - Stitched Herringbone print (center)
    White B - Double Windowpane print (center)
'Color of the Month':
    Tiny Houndstooth print (corners)
    Stitched Herringbone print (border)
    Windowpane print (border)
    Dots print (border)
    Herringbone print (border)

'Fat Eighth' (11" x 18" or 9" x 22") each for Applique:
Pink print	Yellow print
Blue print	Green print

SMALL QUILT - BINDING:
    ½ yard of print to match 'Color of the Month'
BIG QUILT - BORDERS, BACKING and BATTING:
    See pages 32 - 34.
THREAD:
    White, Pink, Yellow, Blue and Green
    Tan pearl cotton (or 6-ply floss) and a #22 Chenille needle.

Summer/Rose Pink -

Winter/Blue - page 12   Spring/Green - page 24

Four Seasons - Quilt Assembly

4 Seasons
4 in 1 – Block of the Month

FINISHED SIZE:
    Wall-Baby-Small size Quilt with pieced border 36" x 48"
    Lap Quilt with pieced border 46" x 74"
    Large Lap Quilt with pieced border 52" x 76"
    Single Quilt with pieced border and 6" border 72" x 96"
    Queen Quilt with pieced border and 6" border 88" x 112"
Note: See pages 32 - 34 for assembly instructions for larger quilts.

Fabric is from www.maywoodstudio.com or www.eeschenck.com

Design Originals   For a color catalog featuring over 200 terrific 'How-To' books, **visit www.d-originals.com**

© 2008 DESIGN ORIGINALS by *Suzanne McNeill*, 2425 Cullen St, Fort Worth, Texas 76107, U.S.A., 817-877-0067 • www.d-originals.com

Summer
Wall or Baby Quilt

Instructions for Summer are on pages 4 - 8.

Summer - Rose Pink

Warm rose and pink colors soften this quilt celebrating the cool romantic moonlit nights of summer. Bright flowers and welcoming vacation homes capture the memories of our favorite season. It's time to travel, luxuriate in the sunshine, relax, and indulge in the pleasures of life - especially sewing.

Enjoy the lazy, hazy days of summer with a quilt that is sure to become a family favorite, at the beach, on vacation, and definitely on the back porch swing.

FINISHED SIZE: 36" x 48"

MATERIALS FOR SUMMER:
SMALL QUILT
'Color of the Month' - Rose Pink

Fat quarter (18" x 22") each for Piecing:
White A - Stitched Herringbone print (center)
White B - Double Windowpane print (center)
'Color of the Month'
Pink - Tiny Houndstooth print (corners)
Pink - Stitched Herringbone print (border)
Pink - Windowpane print (border)
Pink - Dots print (border)
Pink - Herringbone print (border)

Fat eighth (11" x 18" or 9" x 22") each for Applique:
Pink print - Tiny Houndstooth
Yellow print - Tiny Houndstooth
Blue print - Basketweave
Green print - Basketweave

SMALL QUILT 36" x 48"
BINDING:
½ yard of Pink - Tiny Houndstooth
BACKING:
1⅝ yards - 44" x 56"
BATTING
44" x 56"
THREAD
for Piecing - White and Pink
for Applique - Pink, Yellow, Blue and Green

FOR BIG QUILT - BORDERS, BINDING and BACKING:
Lap Quilt with 4" border 46" x 74"
Large Lap Quilt with 4" border 52" x 76"
Single Bed Quilt with 6" border 68" x 84"
Queen Quilt with 6" border 88" x 112"
See pages 32 - 34

Summer

Color for Summer - Rose Pink borders

CENTER:
  Block C1 - cut 2 - 8½" x 16½" (1 of White A, 1 of White B)
  Block A1 - cut 1 - 6½" x 12½" White A
  Block B1 - cut 1 - 11½" x 12½" White B

Use White leftovers for piecing
  Block D1 - cut 1 for B8 - 2" x 15½" White
  Block D1 - cut 2, for A3 and B6 - 2" x 5" White
  Block D1 - cut 2, for A1 and A5 - 2" x 3½" White
  Block D1 - cut 1 for C18 - 2" x 2" White

Pink Color:
  Block D1 - cut 2, for B7 and C16 - 2" x 11" Pink
  Block D1 - cut 2, for C12 and C13 - 2" x 9½" Pink
  Block D1 - cut 2, for C20 and C11 - 2" x 5" Pink
  Block D1 - cut 2, for A2 and C9 - 2" x 2" Pink

Blue Color:
  Block D1 - cut 1 for C14 - 2" x 9½" Blue
  Block D1 - cut 1 for C19 - 2" x 8" Blue
  Block D1 - cut 3, for A4, C15, C17 - 2" x 6½" Blue
  Block D1 - cut 1 for C10 - 2" x 3½" Blue

Green Color:
  Block C1 - cut 1 for long stem - 1" x 18" Green

A1 - Hearts Block

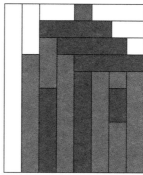

D1 - House Block

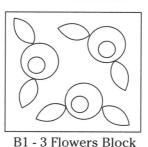

B1 - 3 Flowers Block

C1 - Tall Flower Block

PIECE THE HOUSE BLOCK - D1:
Position the cut pieces for
  the House Block - D1.
Section 1:
  Sew A1 to A2 to A3. Press.
  Sew A4 to A5. Press.
  Sew A 1-2-3 to A 4-5. Press.
Section 2:
  Sew B6 to B7. Press.
  Sew B 6-7 to B8. Press.
Section 3:
  Sew C9 to C10 to C11. Press.
  Sew C 9-10-11 to C12. Press.
  Sew C 9-12 to C13. Press.
  Sew C 9-13 to C14. Press.

Begin adding the roof.
  Sew C 9-14 to C15. Press.
  Sew C 9-15 to C16. Press.
  Sew C17 to C18. Press.
  Sew C 9-16 to C17-18. Press.
  Sew C19 to C20. Press.
  Sew C 9-18 to C19-20. Press.

Assemble the House.
  Sew Section 1 to the top of the house. Press.
  Sew Sew Section 2 to the side of the house. Press.

D1 - House Block

Summer continued

C1- Summer - Petal Q
Cut 1 Yellow
Allow a scant ¼" to turn the edges under.

C1 - Summer
Leaf T

Cut 5 Green
(3 left and 2 right
Allow a scant ¼" to turn
the edges under.

Position
C1 - Summer
Petal R
and
C1 - Summer
Petals Center S
here

B1 - Summer
Flower Center W

Cut 3 Pink
Allow a scant ¼" to
turn the edges
under.

B1 - Summer
Leaf V

Cut 6 Green
Allow a scant ¼" to turn
the edges under.

Summer
Flower
Panel

Cut 2
(1 from
White A
and
1 from
White B)

A1 - Summer - Heart P

Cut 2 Pink
Allow a scant ¼" to turn the edges under.

C1 - Tall Flower Block

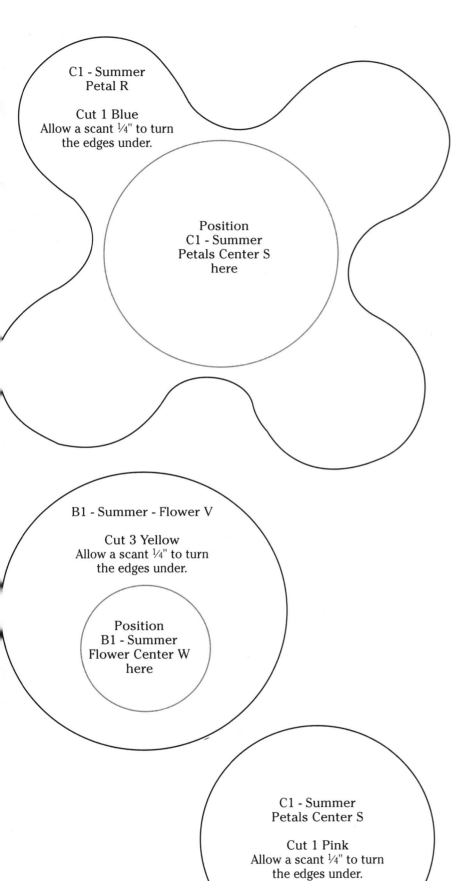

C1 - Summer
Petal R

Cut 1 Blue
Allow a scant ¼" to turn
the edges under.

Position
C1 - Summer
Petals Center S
here

B1 - Summer - Flower V

Cut 3 Yellow
Allow a scant ¼" to turn
the edges under.

Position
B1 - Summer
Flower Center W
here

C1 - Summer
Petals Center S

Cut 1 Pink
Allow a scant ¼" to turn
the edges under.

ASSEMBLE BLOCKS:
Assemble the 4 blocks as shown on pages 4 and 5.

APPLIQUE THE DESIGN BLOCKS - A1, B1 and C1:
    Cut out the designs.
    Applique the pieces in the method of your
    choice, see page 10.

BORDER - MODIFIED LOG CABIN BLOCKS:
    Small Quilt:

PREPARATION FOR BLOCKS
    #1 - Cut 12 - 4½" x 4½" from darkest print.
    #2 - Cut 12 - 2½" x 4½" from dots print.
    #3 - Cut 12 - 2½" x 6½" from dots print.
    #4a - Cut 6 - 2½" x 6½" from windowpane print.
    #4b - Cut 6 - 2½" x 6½" from herringbone print.
    #5a - Cut 6 - 2½" x 8½" from windowpane print.
    #5b - Cut 6 - 2½" x 8½" from herringbone print.
Note: 4a and 5a should be used in the same block.
        4b and 5b should be used in the same block.

 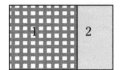

Sew strip (2) to square (1).

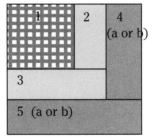

Modified Log Cabin Assembly

SEW THE BLOCKS:
    See the Modified Log Cabin Block for
        placement.
    For each block, sew #1 to #2. Press.
    Sew #3 to the bottom of the block. Press.
    Sew #4 to the right side of the block. Press.
Note: 4a and 5a should be used in the same block.
        4b and 5b should be used in the same block.
    Sew #5 to the bottom of the block. Press.
    Each block will measure 8½" x 8½" at this point.

Summer continued

FOR SMALL QUILT BORDER
Each Border block will measure 8" x 8" finished.

Center Strips for Top and Bottom Borders:
From leftover Pink, cut 4 strips 2½" x 8½".

Corner Squares:
From darkest print, cut 4 squares 8½" x 8½".

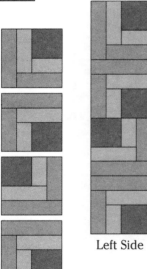

Left Side   Right Side

6 Blocks

Position blocks around the center for desired color placement.

Side Borders:
Sew 4 blocks together for the side rows.
Make 2. Press.

1 corner square - 1 block - 2 strips - 1 block - 1 square

Top Border

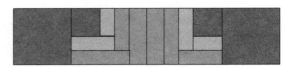

Bottom Border

Top and Bottom Borders:
Sew the following:
1 corner square - 1 block - 2 strips - 1 block - 1 square together for the top and bottom borders. Press.

SMALL QUILT BORDER
Sew side borders to the quilt center.
Sew top and bottom borders to the quilt. Press.

BINDING:
Cut strips 2½" wide.
Sew together end to end to equal 178".
See Binding Instructions on page 11.

OR FOR LARGE QUILT and BORDER - see pages 32 - 34.

Tips for Working with 'Fat Quarters' and Pieces

TIPS: As a Guide for Yardage:
Each 1/4 yard or a 'Fat Quarter' equals 18" x 22".
Each 1/8 yard or a 'Fat Eighth' equals 11" x 18".

Pre-cut bundles of 'Fat Quarter' and 'Fat Eighth' cuts make fabric planning easy.

Packaged kits and bundles contain all the fabric you need for 1 quilt top.

You only need to add the binding, backing, batting and threads.

1. Pre-cut pieces for piecing and applique are cut with the grain going in different directions and may be prone to stretching.

Do not wash pieces or cuts of fabric because the edges will ravel and they will stretch out of shape. After they are quilted to a backing, they are stable.

These tips will help reduce stretching and make your quilt lay flat for quilting.

2. When sewing crosswise grain pieces together, take care not to stretch the pieces. If you detect any puckering as you go, rip out the seam and sew it again.

3. Press, Do Not Iron. Carefully open fabric, with the seam to one side, press without moving the iron. A back-and-forth ironing motion stretches the fabric.

4. Reduce the wiggle in your borders with this technique from garment making.

First, accurately cut your borders to the exact measure of the quilt top. Then, before sewing the border to the quilt, run a double row of stay stitches along the outside edge to maintain the original shape and prevent stretching.

Pin the border to the quilt, taking care not to stretch the quilt top to make it fit. Pinning reduces slipping and stretching.

Rotary Cutting Tips

Rotary Cutter: Friend or Foe

A rotary cutter is wonderful and useful. When not used correctly, the sharp blade can be a dangerous tool. Follow these safety tips:

1. Never cut toward you.

2. Use a sharp blade. Pressing harder on a dull blade can cause the blade to jump the ruler and injure your fingers.

3. Always disengage the blade before the cutter leaves your hand, even if you intend to pick it up immediately.

Rotary cutters have been caught when lifting fabric, have fallen onto the floor and have cut fingers.

Basic Sewing Instructions

You now have precisely cut strips that are exactly the correct width. You are well on your way to blocks that fit together perfectly. Accurate sewing is the next important step.

Matching Edges:

1. Carefully line up the edges of your strips. Many times, if the underside is off a little, your seam will be off by 1/8". This does not sound like much until you have 8 seams in a block, each off by 1/8". Now your finished block is a whole inch wrong!

2. Pin the pieces together to prevent them shifting.

Seam Allowance:

I cannot stress enough the importance of accurate 1/4" seams. All the quilts in this book are measured for 1/4" seams unless otherwise indicated.

Most sewing machine manufacturers offer a Quarter-inch foot. A Quarter-inch foot is the most worthwhile investment you can make in your quilting.

Pressing:

I want to talk about pressing even before we get to sewing because proper pressing can make the difference between a quilt that wins a ribbon at the quilt show and one that does not.

Press, do NOT iron. What does that mean? Many of us want to move the iron back and forth along the seam. This "ironing" stretches the strip out of shape and creates errors that accumulate as the quilt is constructed. Believe it or not, there is a correct way to press your seams, and here it is:

1. Do NOT use steam with your iron. If you need a little water, spritz it on.

2. Place your fabric flat on the ironing board without opening the seam. Set a hot iron on the seam and count to 3. Lift the iron and move to the next position along the seam. Repeat until the entire seam is pressed. This sets and sinks the threads into the fabric.

3. Now, carefully lift the top strip and fold it away from you so the seam is on one side. Usually the seam is pressed toward the darker fabric, but often the direction of the seam is determined by the piecing requirements.

4. Press the seam open with your fingers. Add a little water or spray starch if it wants to close again. Lift the iron and place it on the seam. Count to 3. Lift the iron again and continue until the seam is pressed. Do NOT use the tip of the iron to push the seam open. So many people do this and wonder later why their blocks are not fitting together.

5. Most critical of all: For accuracy every seam must be pressed before the next seam is sewn.

Working with 'Crosswise Grain' strips:

Strips cut on the crosswise grain (from selvage to selvage) have problems similar to bias edges and are prone to stretching. To reduce stretching and make your quilt lay flat for quilting, keep these tips in mind.

1. Take care not to stretch the strips as you sew.

2. Adjust the sewing thread tension and the presser foot pressure if needed.

3. If you detect any puckering as you go, rip out the seam and sew it again. It is much easier to take out a seam now than to do it after the block is sewn.

continued on page 10

Sewing Bias Edges:

Bias edges wiggle and stretch out of shape very easily. They are not recommended for beginners, but even a novice can accomplish bias edges if these techniques are employed.

1. Stabilize the bias edge with one of these methods:

    a) Press with spray starch.

    b) Press freezer paper or removable iron-on stabilizer to the back of the fabric.

    c) Sew a double row of stay stitches along the bias edge and ⅛" from the bias edge. This is a favorite technique of garment makers.

2. Pin, pin, pin! I know many of us dislike pinning, but when working with bias edges, pinning makes the difference between intersections that match and those that do not.

Building Better Borders:

Wiggly borders make a quilt very difficult to finish. However, wiggly borders can be avoided with these techniques.

1. Cut the borders on grain. That means cutting your strips parallel to the selvage edge.

2. Accurately cut your borders to the exact measure of the quilt.

3. If your borders are piece stripped from crosswise grain fabrics, press well with spray starch and sew a double row of stay stitches along the outside edge to maintain the original shape and prevent stretching.

4. Pin the border to the quilt, taking care not to stretch the quilt top to make it fit. Pinning reduces slipping and stretching.

Embroidery Use 24" lengths of doubled pearl cotton or 6-ply floss and a #22 or #24 Chenille needle (this needle has a large eye). Outline large elements.

 *Running Stitch* Come up at A. Weave the needle through the fabric, making LONG stitches on the top and SHORT stitches on the bottom. Keep stitches even.

Basic Layering Instructions

Marking Your Quilt:

If you choose to mark your quilt for hand or machine quilting, it is much easier to do so before layering. Press your quilt before you begin. Here are some handy tips regarding marking.

1. A disappearing pen may vanish before you finish.

2. Use a White pencil on dark fabrics.

3. If using a washable Blue pen, remember that pressing may make the pen permanent.

Pieced Backings:

1. Press the backing fabric before measuring.

2. If possible cut backing fabrics on grain, parallel to the selvage edges.

3. Piece 3 parts rather than 2 whenever possible, sewing 2 side borders to the center. This reduces stress on the pieced seam.

4. The backing and batting should extend at least 2" on each side of the quilt.

Creating a Quilt Sandwich:

1. Press the backing and top to remove all wrinkles.

2. Lay the backing wrong side up on the table.

3. Position the batting over the backing and smooth out all wrinkles.

4. Center the quilt top over the batting leaving a 2" border all around.

5. Pin the layers together with 2" safety pins positioned a handwidth apart. A grapefruit spoon makes inserting the pins easier. Leaving the pins open in the container speeds up the basting on the next quilt.

Applique Instructions

Basic Turned Edge:

1. Trace pattern onto template plastic.

2. Cut out the shape leaving a scant ¼" fabric border all around and clip the curves.

3. Place the template plastic on the wrong side of the fabric. Spray edges with starch.

4. Press the ⅛" border over the edge of the template plastic with the tip of a hot iron. Press firmly.

5. Remove the template, maintaining the folded edge on the back of the fabric.

6. Position the shape on the quilt and Blindstitch in place.

Basic Needle Turn:

1. Cut out the shape leaving a ¼" fabric border all around.

2. Baste the shapes to the quilt, keeping the basting stitches away from the edge of the fabric.

3. Begin with all areas that are under other layers and work to the topmost layer.

4. For an area no more than 2" ahead of where you are working, trim to ⅛" and clip the curves.

5. Using the needle, roll the edge under and sew tiny Blindstitches to secure.

Using Fusible Web for Iron-on Applique:

1. Trace the pattern onto *Steam a Seam 2* fusible web.

2. Press the patterns onto the wrong side of the fabric.

3. Cut out patterns exactly on the drawn line.

4. Score the web paper with a pin, then remove the paper.

5. Position the fabric, fusible side down, on the quilt. Press with a hot iron following the fusible web manufacturer's instructions.

6. Stitch around the edge by hand.

Optional: Stabilize the wrong side of the fabric with your favorite stabilizer.

Use a size 80 machine embroidery needle. Fill the bobbin with lightweight basting thread and thread the machine with a machine embroidery thread that complements the color being appliqued.

Set your machine for a Zigzag stitch and adjust the thread tension if needed. Use a scrap to experiment with different stitch widths and lengths until you find the one you like best.

Sew slowly.

Basic Quilting Instructions

Hand Quilting:

Many quilters enjoy the serenity of hand quilting. Because the quilt is handled a great deal, it is important to securely baste the sandwich together. Place the quilt in a hoop and don't forget to hide your knots.

Machine Quilting:

All the quilts in this book were machine quilted. Some were quilted on a large, free-arm quilting machine and others were quilted on a sewing machine. If you have never machine quilted before, practice on some scraps first.

Straight Line Machine Quilting Tips:

1. Pin baste the layers securely.

2. Set up your sewing machine with a size 80 quilting needle and a walking foot.

3. Experimenting with the decorative stitches on your machine adds interest to your quilt. You do not have to quilt the entire piece with the same stitch. Variety is the spice of life, so have fun trying out stitches you have never used before as well as your favorite stand-bys.

Free Motion Machine Quilting Tips:

1. Pin baste the layers securely.

2. Set up your sewing machine with a spring needle, a quilting foot, and lower the feed dogs.

Basic Mitered Binding Instructions

A Perfect Finish:

The binding endures the most stress on a quilt and is usually the first thing to wear out. For this reason, we recommend using a double fold binding.

1. Trim the backing and batting even with the quilt edge.

2. If possible cut strips on the crosswise grain because a little bias in the binding is a Good thing. This is the only place in the quilt where bias is helpful, for it allows the binding to give as it is turned to the back and sewn in place.

3. Strips are usually cut 2½" wide, but check the instructions for your project before cutting.

4. Sew strips end to end to make a long strip sufficient to go all around the quilt plus 4"- 6".

5. With wrong sides together, fold the strip in half lengthwise. Press.

6. Stretch out your hand and place your little finger at the corner of the quilt top. Place the binding where your thumb touches the edge of the quilt. Aligning the edge of the quilt with the raw edges of the binding, pin the binding in place along the first side.

7. Leaving a 2" tail for later use, begin sewing the binding to the quilt with a ¼" seam.

For Mitered Corners:

1. Stop ¼" from the first corner. Leave the needle in the quilt and turn it 90°. Hit the reverse button on your machine and back off the quilt leaving the threads connected.

2. Fold the binding perpendicular to the side you sewed, making a 45° angle. Carefully maintaining the first fold, bring the binding back along the edge to be sewn.

3. Carefully align the edges of the binding with the quilt edge and sew as you did the first side. Repeat this process until you reach the tail left at the beginning. Fold the tail out of the way and sew until you are ¼" from the beginning stitches.

4. Remove the quilt from the machine. Fold the quilt out of the way and match the binding tails together. Carefully sew the binding tails with a ¼" seam. You can do this by hand if you prefer.

Finishing the Binding:

5. Trim the seam to reduce bulk.

6. Finish stitching the binding to the quilt across the join you just sewed.

7. Turn the binding to the back of the quilt. To reduce bulk at the corners, fold the miter in the opposite direction from which it was folded on the front.

8. Hand-sew a Blind stitch on the back of the quilt to secure the binding in place.

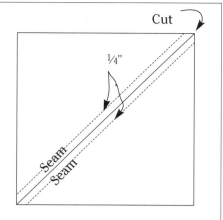

Half-Square Triangle Diagram
1. Place 2 squares right sides together.
2. Draw a diagonal line from corner to corner.
3. Stitch ¼" on each side of the line.
4. Cut squares apart on the diagonal line.
5. Open the 2 new squares with 2 colors.
6. Press. Trim off dog-ears.
7. Center and trim to size.

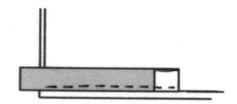

Align the raw edge of the binding with the raw edge of the quilt top. Start about 8" from the corner and go along the first side with a ¼" seam.

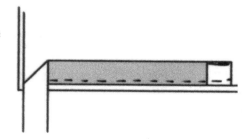

Stop ¼" from the edge. Then stitch a slant to the corner (through both layers of binding)... lift up, then down, as you line up the edge. Fold the binding back.

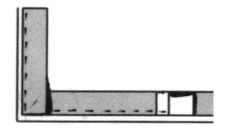

Align the raw edge again. Continue stitching the next side with a ¼" seam as you sew the binding in place.

Winter - Blue

Winter
Wall or Baby Quilt

Instructions for Winter are on pages 12 - 17.

Cool colors hint at the frost and coming snows. Blue-gray skies remind us that this is the perfect time to keep snug in your sewing room making a new flannel quilt.

You will enjoy the chilly months much more when you surround yourself with sumptuous soft fabrics while making beautiful quilts for your family and friends.

FINISHED SIZE: 36" x 48"

MATERIALS FOR WINTER:
    SMALL QUILT
    'Color of the Month' - Blue

Fat quarter (18" x 22") each for Piecing:
        White A - Stitched Herringbone (center)
        White B - Double Windowpane (center)
    'Color of the Month'
        Blue - Tiny Houndstooth print (corners)
        Blue - Stitched Herringbone print (border)
        Blue - Windowpane print (border)
        Blue - Dots print (border)
        Blue - Herringbone print (border)

Fat eighth (11" x 18" or 9" x 22") each for Applique:
        Pink print - Basketweave
        Yellow print - Tiny Houndstooth
        Blue print - Basketweave
        Green print - Tiny Houndstooth

SMALL QUILT 36" x 48"
    BINDING:
        ½ yard of Blue - Tiny Houndstooth
    BACKING:
    1⅝ yards - 44" x 56"
    BATTING
        44" x 56"
    THREAD
        for Piecing - White and Blue
        for Applique - Pink, Yellow, Blue and Green
        for Embroidery - Tan pearl cotton (or 6-ply floss)
        #22 Chenille needle

FOR BIG QUILT - BORDERS, BINDING and BACKING:
    Lap Quilt with 4" border 46" x 74"
    Large Lap Quilt with 4" border 52" x 76"
    Single Bed Quilt with 6" border 68" x 84"
    Queen Quilt with 6" border 88" x 112"
    See pages 32 - 34

Winter

Color for Winter - Blue borders

CENTER:
>Block M1 - cut 1 - 17½" x 20½" of White A
>Block N1 - cut 1 - 8½" x 20½" of White B

Use White leftovers for piecing
>Block O1 - cut 2 for D1 - 3½" x 7½" White
>Block O1 - cut 1 for B2 - 6" x 6" White
>Block O1 - cut 2 for C3 - 2½" x 3½" White
>Block O1 - cut 1 for C1 - 3" x 3" White

Blue Color:
>Block O1 - cut 1 for B1 - 6" x 6" Blue
>Block O1 - cut 1 for C2 - 3" x 3" Blue
>Block O1 - cut 2 for A2 - 2½" x 2½" Blue
>Block O1 - cut 1 for A3 - 2½" x 4½" Blue
>Block O1 - cut 1 for A4 - 3½" x 4½" Blue

Pink Color:
>Block O1 - cut 1 for A1 - 2½" x 4½" Pink

M1 - Folk Flower Block

O1 - Basket Block

N1 - Running Bunny Block

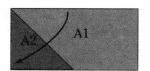

PIECE THE BASKET BLOCK - O1:

Section 1 Center - Use A1, A2, A3 and A4:
>Position one A2 on a corner of A1.
>Draw a diagonal line from corner to corner.
>Sew a seam on the diagonal line.
>Fold the corner down
>Trim off excess fabric underneath piece.
>Press.

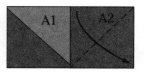

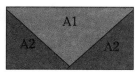

>Position second A2 on another corner of A1.
>Draw a diagonal line from corner to corner.
>Sew a seam on the diagonal line.
>Fold the corner down
>Trim off excess fabric underneath the piece.
>Press.

>Sew A1-2-2 to A3.
>Sew A1-2-3 to A4.

TIP: See instructions for half-square triangle block on page 11.

Section 2 Large Squares on Sides - Use B1 and B2:
>Pair up two 6" x 6" colors together.
>Draw a line from corner to corner on the diagonal.
>Sew a seam ¼" on each side of the diagonal line.
>Cut apart on the diagonal line to make 2 squares. Press.
>Center and trim each half-square triangle block to 5½" x 5½".
>You made 2.

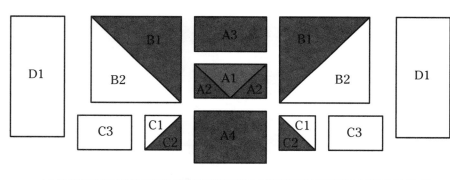

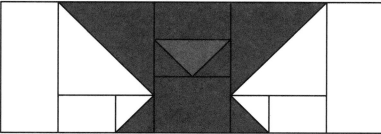

O1 - Basket Block

Section 3 Small squares on Sides - Use C1, C2 and C3:
>Pair up two 3" x 3" colors together.
>Draw a line from corner to corner on the diagonal.
>Sew a seam ¼" on each side of the diagonal line.
>Cut apart on the diagonal line to make 2 squares. Press.
>Center and trim each half-square triangle block to 2½" x 2½". You made 2.

>Sew C1-2 to C3. Make 2, refer to diagram for placement.

Assemble the Basket.
>Sew Section 2 to Section 3. Make 2, refer to diagram for placement.
>Sew Section 1 to Sections 2/3, then sew to D1.
>Sew this piece to Sections 2/3, then sew to D1 on the other side.

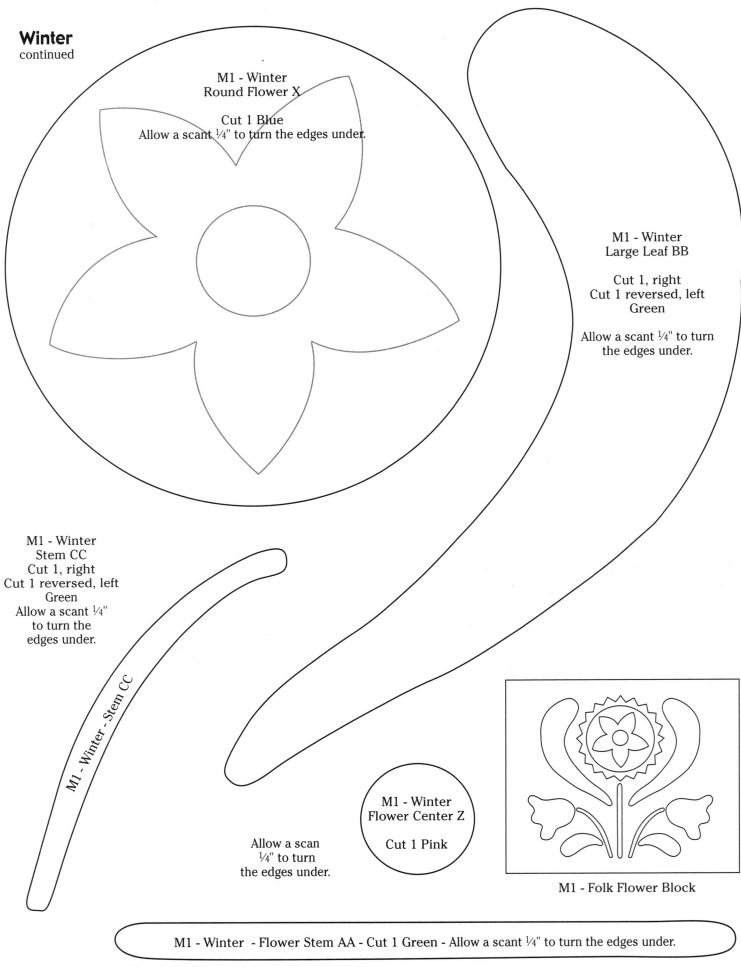

M1 - Winter
Round Flower X

Cut 1 Blue
Allow a scant ¼" to turn the edges under.

M1 - Winter
Large Leaf BB

Cut 1, right
Cut 1 reversed, left
Green

Allow a scant ¼" to turn
the edges under.

M1 - Winter
Stem CC
Cut 1, right
Cut 1 reversed, left
Green
Allow a scant ¼"
to turn the
edges under.

M1 - Winter - Stem CC

Allow a scan
¼" to turn
the edges under.

M1 - Winter
Flower Center Z

Cut 1 Pink

M1 - Folk Flower Block

M1 - Winter - Flower Stem AA - Cut 1 Green - Allow a scant ¼" to turn the edges under.

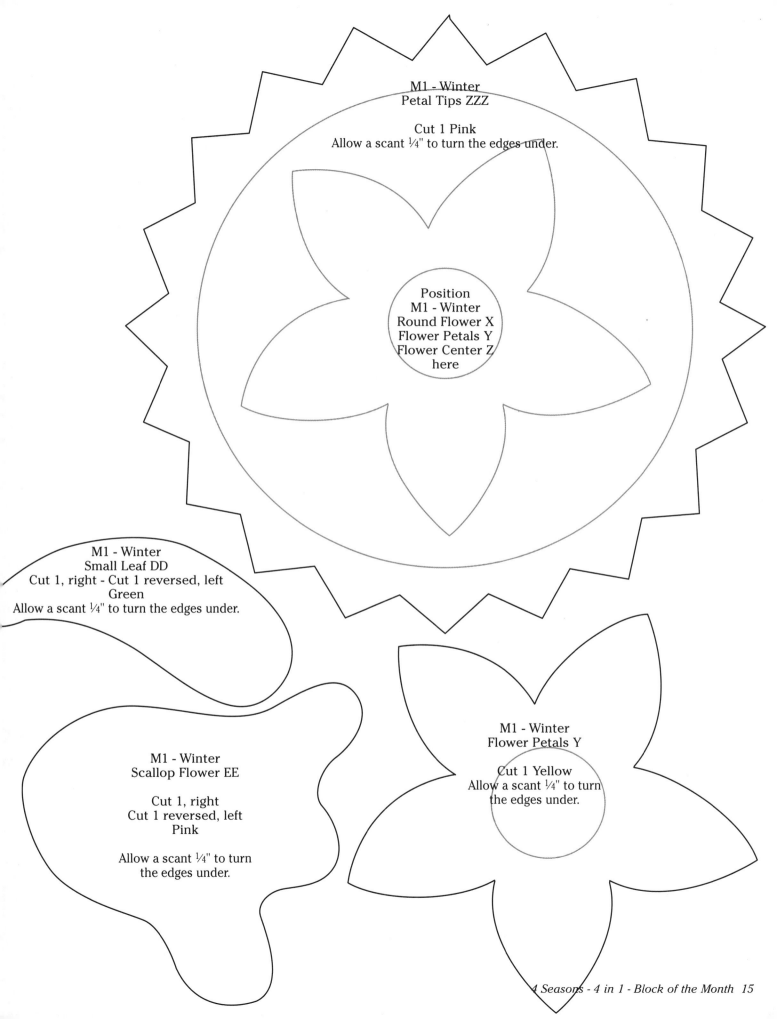

M1 - Winter
Petal Tips ZZZ

Cut 1 Pink
Allow a scant ¼" to turn the edges under.

Position
M1 - Winter
Round Flower X
Flower Petals Y
Flower Center Z
here

M1 - Winter
Small Leaf DD
Cut 1, right - Cut 1 reversed, left
Green
Allow a scant ¼" to turn the edges under.

M1 - Winter
Scallop Flower EE

Cut 1, right
Cut 1 reversed, left
Pink

Allow a scant ¼" to turn
the edges under.

M1 - Winter
Flower Petals Y

Cut 1 Yellow
Allow a scant ¼" to turn
the edges under.

ASSEMBLE BLOCKS:
Assemble the 3 blocks as shown on pages 12 and 13.

APPLIQUE THE DESIGN BLOCKS - M1 and N1:
Cut out the designs.
Applique the pieces in the method of your choice, see page 10.
Embroider an eye with Tan pearl cotton (or 6-ply floss) and a #22 Chenille needle.

Each pair of squares will make 2 half-square triangles

TIP: See instructions for half-square triangle block on page 11.

BORDER - HALF-SQUARE TRIANGLE BLOCKS:

Small Quilt:
Cut 12 - 9" x 9" squares
Pair up colors together (a light and a dark).
Draw a line from corner to corner on the diagonal.
Sew a seam ¼" on each side of the diagonal line.
Cut apart on the diagonal line to make 2 squares.
Press.
Trim each half-square triangle block to 8½" x 8½".
Make 12.

Single 4 Seasons Quilt: Make 6 half-square triangle blocks.
(see page 34).

N1 - Running Bunny Block

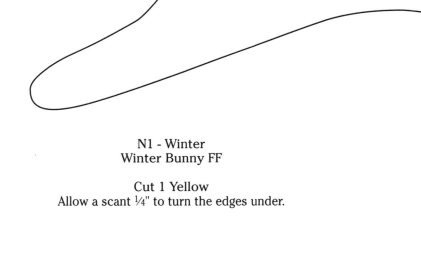

N1 - Winter
Winter Bunny FF

Cut 1 Yellow
Allow a scant ¼" to turn the edges under.

FOR SMALL QUILT BORDER
Each Border block will measure 8" x 8" finished.

 Center Strips for Top and Bottom Borders:
From leftover colors cut 2 - 4½" x 8½".

 Corner Squares:
Cut 4 squares - 8½" x 8½."

4 Blocks   Left Side   Right Side
(Turn the Left Side
upside down)

Position blocks around the center for desired color placement.

Side Borders:
Sew 4 blocks together for the side rows. Make 2. Press.

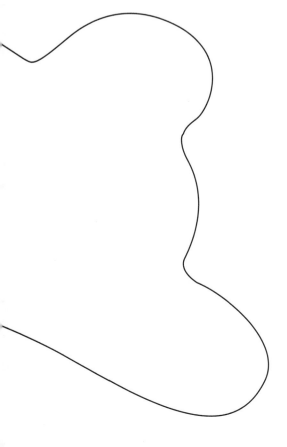

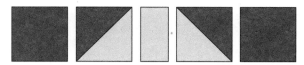

1 corner square - 1 block - 1 strip - 1 block - 1 square

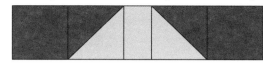

Top Border

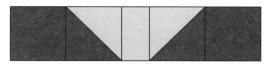

Bottom Border
(Turn the Top Border upside down)

Top and Bottom Borders:
Sew the following:
1 corner square - 1 block - 1 strip - 1 block - 1 square
together for the top and bottom borders. Press.

SMALL QUILT BORDER
Sew side borders to the quilt center.
Sew top and bottom borders to the quilt. Press.

BINDING:
Cut strips 2½" wide.
Sew together end to end to equal 178".
See Binding Instructions on page 11.

OR FOR LARGE QUILT and BORDER - see pages 32 - 34.

Fall - Yellow

Fall
Wall or Baby Quilt

Instructions for Fall are on pages 18 - 23.

Golden harvest colors create a festive backdrop for these fabulous blocks which provide the perfect opportunity to practice simple piecing skills and easy appliques.

Celebrate the season of thanks by sharing your sewing skills with someone you love or join one of the many community comfort quilting projects making charity blankets for hospitals and nursing homes, orphanages and homeless shelters.

FINISHED SIZE: 36" x 48"

MATERIALS FOR FALL:
    SMALL QUILT
    'Color of the Month' - Yellow

Fat quarter (18" x 22") each for Piecing:
        White A - Stitched Herringbone print (center)
        White B - Double Windowpane print (center)
    'Color of the Month'
        Yellow - Tiny Houndstooth print (corners)
        Yellow - Stitched Herringbone print (border)
        Yellow - Windowpane print (border)
        Yellow - Dots print (border)
        Yellow - Herringbone print (border)

Fat eighth (11" x 18" or 9" x 22") each for Applique:
        Pink print - tiny Houndstooth
        Yellow print - Tiny Houndstooth
        Blue print - Basketweave
        Green print - Basketweave

SMALL QUILT 36" x 48"
    BINDING:
        ½ yard of Yellow - Tiny Houndstooth
    BACKING:
        1⅝ yards - 44" x 56"
    BATTING
        44" x 56"
    THREAD
        for Piecing - White and Yellow
        for Applique - Pink, Yellow, Blue and Green
        for Embroidery - Tan pearl cotton (or 6-ply floss)
        #22 Chenille needle.

FOR BIG QUILT - BORDERS, BINDING and BACKING:
    Lap Quilt with 4" border 46" x 74"
    Large Lap Quilt with 4" border 52" x 76"
    Single Bed Quilt with 6" border 68" x 84"
    Queen Quilt with 6" border 88" x 112"
    See pages 32 - 34

Fall

Color for Fall - Yellow borders

CENTER:
  Block E1 - cut 1 - 10½" x 12½" of White A
  Block F1 - cut 1 - 8½" x 10½" of White A
  Block G1 - cut 1 - 11½" x 12½" of White B
  Block H1 - cut 1 - 8½" x 12½" of White B

Use White leftovers for piecing::
  Block J1 - cut 2 - 5" x 5" White
  Block L1 - cut 2 - 2½" x 15" White

Color:
  Block I1 - cut 2 - 4" x 4" Yellow
  Block I1 - cut 2 - 4" x 4" Blue
  Block J1 - cut 2 - 5" x 5" Blue
  Block K1 - cut 1 - 2½" x 8½" Green
  Block L1 - cut 2 - 2½" x 15" Pink

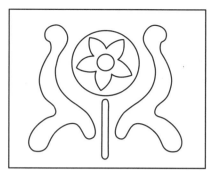

E1 - Round Flower Block

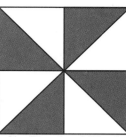

J1 - Pinwheel Block

I 1 - Triangles Block

F1 - Tulip Block

G1 - Berries Block

K1 - Color Block

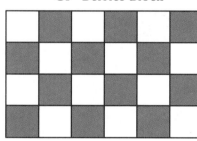

L1 - Checkerboard Block

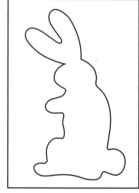

H1 - Bunny Block

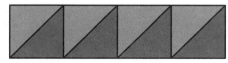

I 1 - Triangles Block

TIP: See instructions for half-square triangle block on page 11.

I1 - TRIANGLES BLOCK
  Use two 4" x 4" Yellow and two 4" x 4" Blue
  Pair up two 4" x 4" color squares together
    (1 Blue and 1 Yellow).
  Draw a line from corner to corner on the diagonal.
  Sew a seam ¼" on each side of the diagonal line.
  Cut apart on the diagonal line to make 2 squares. Press.
  Center & trim each half-square triangle block to 3½" x 3½".
  Make 4.

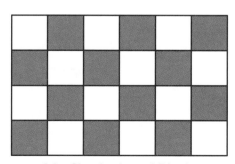

L1 - Checkerboard Block

L1 - CHECKERBOARD BLOCK
  Use two 2½" x 15" White and two 2½" x 15" Pink.
  Sew 4 strips together side by side:
    White - Pink - White - Pink.
  Cut sewn strips into 6 sections, each 2½" x 8½"
  Position strips in the checkerboard pattern.
  Sew together to make the checkerboard. Press.

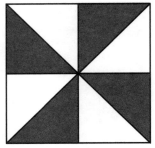

J1 - Pinwheel Block

TIP: See instructions for half-square triangle block on page 11.

I1 - PINWHEEL BLOCK
    Use two 5" x 5" White and two 5" x 5" Blue.
    Pair up two 5" x 5" color squares together
        (1 White and 1 Blue).
    Draw a line from corner to corner on the diagonal.
    Sew a seam ¼" on each side of the diagonal line.
    Cut apart on the diagonal line to make 2 squares. Press.
    Center & trim each half-square triangle block to 4½" x 4½".
    Make 4.

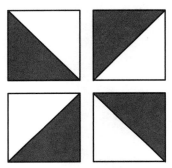

J1 - Pinwheel Block

Position blocks into a square, note the position.
Sew the blocks together. Press.
Finished block is 8½" x 8½".
Make 1.

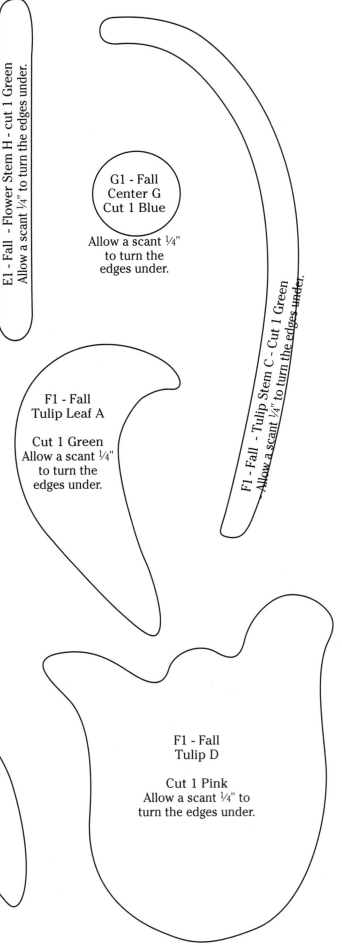

E1 - Fall - Flower Stem H - cut 1 Green
Allow a scant ¼" to turn the edges under.

G1 - Fall
Center G
Cut 1 Blue

Allow a scant ¼"
to turn the
edges under.

F1 - Fall - Tulip Stem C - Cut 1 Green
Allow a scant ¼" to turn the edges under.

F1 - Fall
Tulip Leaf A

Cut 1 Green
Allow a scant ¼"
to turn the
edges under.

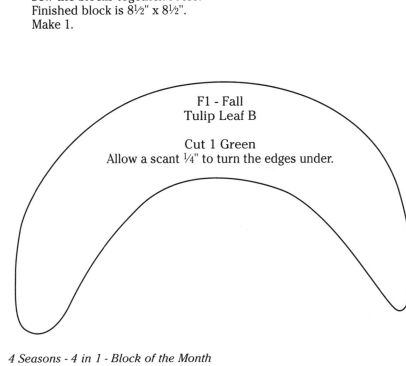

F1 - Fall
Tulip Leaf B

Cut 1 Green
Allow a scant ¼" to turn the edges under.

F1 - Fall
Tulip D

Cut 1 Pink
Allow a scant ¼" to
turn the edges under.

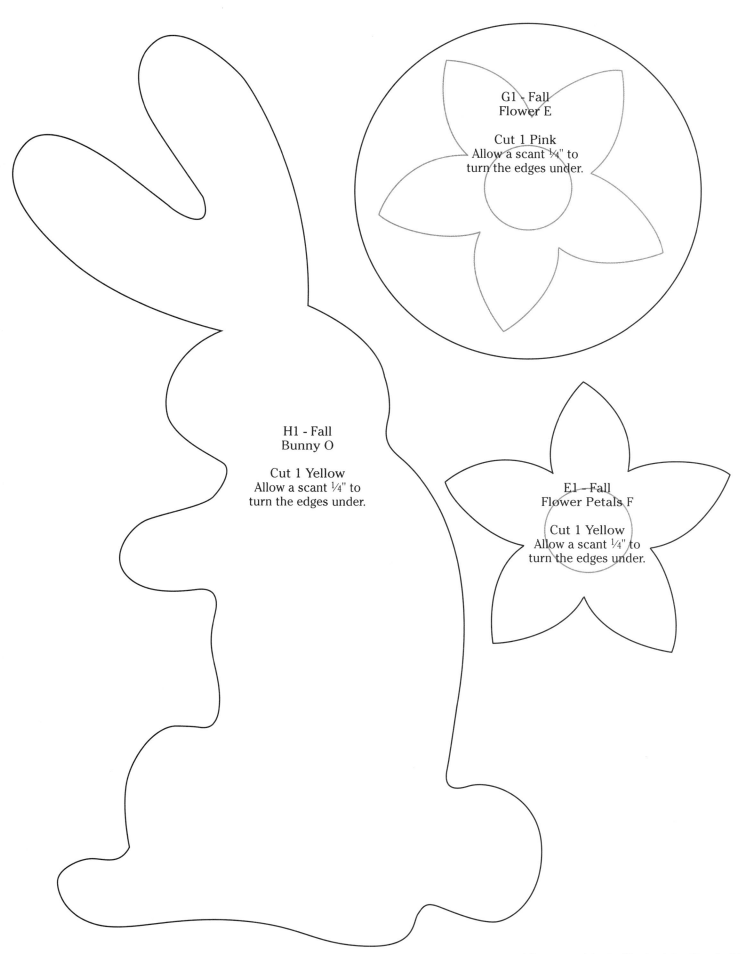

G1 - Fall
Flower E

Cut 1 Pink
Allow a scant ¼" to
turn the edges under.

H1 - Fall
Bunny O

Cut 1 Yellow
Allow a scant ¼" to
turn the edges under.

E1 - Fall
Flower Petals F

Cut 1 Yellow
Allow a scant ¼" to
turn the edges under.

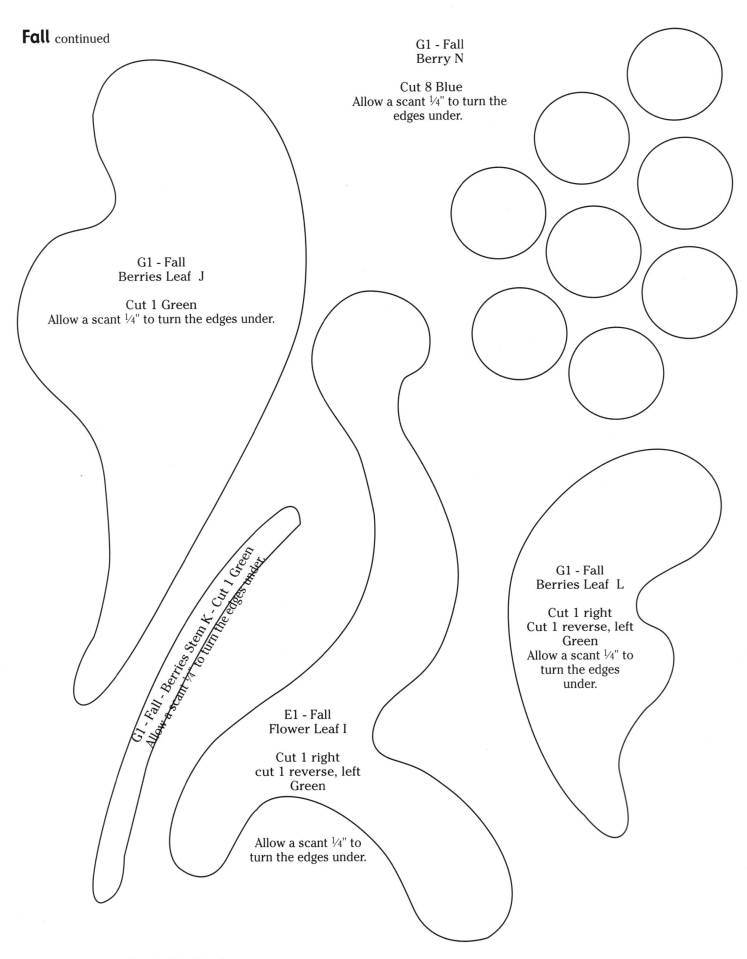

G1 - Fall
Berry N

Cut 8 Blue
Allow a scant ¼" to turn the
edges under.

G1 - Fall
Berries Leaf J

Cut 1 Green
Allow a scant ¼" to turn the edges under.

G1 - Fall - Berries Stem K - Cut 1 Green
Allow a scant ¼" to turn the edges under.

G1 - Fall
Berries Leaf L

Cut 1 right
Cut 1 reverse, left
Green
Allow a scant ¼" to
turn the edges
under.

E1 - Fall
Flower Leaf I

Cut 1 right
cut 1 reverse, left
Green

Allow a scant ¼" to
turn the edges under.

ASSEMBLE BLOCKS:
Assemble the 8 blocks as shown on pages 18 and 19.

APPLIQUE THE DESIGN BLOCKS - E1, F1, G1, H1:
Cut out the designs.
Applique the pieces in the method of your choice, see page 10.
Embroider an eye with Tan pearl cotton (or 6-ply floss) and a #22 Chenille needle.

BORDER - PIANO KEY BLOCKS:
  Small Quilt:
      Cut 52 - 2½" x 8½" strips.
      Sew strips together side by side.
  Single 4 Seasons Quilt:
      Make 1 set of 10 and 1 set of 16 piano keys (see page 34).
  Queen 4 Seasons Quilt:
      Make 1 set of 10, 1 set of 14, 1 set of 16 and 1 set of 20 piano keys. (see pages 33-34).

FOR SMALL QUILT BORDER

Corner Squares:
      Cut 4 squares - 8½" x 8½."

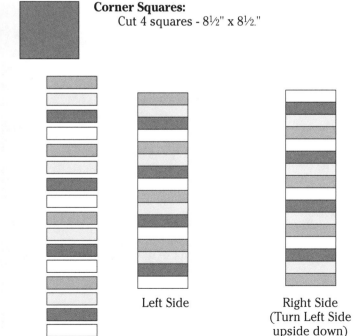

Left Side

Right Side
(Turn Left Side
upside down)

16 strips

Position strips around the center for desired color placement.
Side Borders:
      Sew 16 strips together side by side for the side rows.
      Make 2. Press.

1 corner square - 10 strips - 1 corner square

Top Border

Bottom Border
(Turn Top Border upside down)

Top and Bottom Borders:

Sew the following:
      1 corner square - 10 strips - 1 corner square
      together for the top and bottom borders. Press.

SMALL QUILT BORDER
      Sew side borders to the quilt center. Press.
      Sew top and bottom borders to the quilt. Press.

BINDING:
      Cut strips 2½" wide.
      Sew together end to end to equal 178".
      See Binding Instructions on page 11.

OR FOR LARGE QUILT and BORDER - see pages 32 - 34.

Spring - Green

Spring
Wall or Baby Quilt

Instructions for Spring are on pages 24 - 32.

The grass is turning green. The birds are nesting in the budding trees. The flowers are coming up in the garden, and the butterflies are making their first appearance of the year. It must be Spring!

Rejuvenate your sewing spirit with a verdant quilt that promises all things bright and beautiful.

FINISHED SIZE: 36" x 48"

MATERIALS FOR SPRING:
     SMALL QUILT
          'Color of the Month' - Green

Fat quarter (18" x 22") each for Piecing:
          White A - Stitched Herringbone print (center)
          White B - Double Windowpane print (center)
          'Color of the Month'
          Green - Tiny Houndstooth print (corners)
          Green - Stitched Herringbone print (border)
          Green - Windowpane print (border)
          Green - Dots print (border)
          Green - Herringbone print (border)

Fat eighth (11" x 18" or 9" x 22") each for Applique:
          Pink print - Basketweave
          Yellow print - Tiny Houndstooth
          Blue print - Basketweave
          Green print - Tiny Houndstooth

SMALL QUILT 36" x 48"
     BINDING:
          ½ yard of Green - Tiny Houndstooth
     BACKING:
          1⅝ yards - 44" x 56"
     BATTING
          44" x 56"
     THREAD
          for Piecing - White and Green
          for Applique - Pink, Yellow, Blue and Green
          for Embroidery - Tan pearl cotton (or 6-ply floss)
          #22 Chenille needle.

FOR BIG QUILT - BORDERS, BINDING and BACKING:
     Lap Quilt with 4" border 46" x 74"
     Large Lap Quilt with 4" border 52" x 76"
     Single Bed Quilt with 6" border 68" x 84"
     Queen Quilt with 6" border 88" x 112"
     See pages 32 - 34

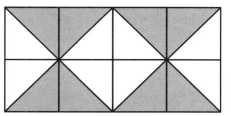

U1 - Hourglass Block

P1 - Bluebird Block

S1 - Color A Block

T1 - Color B Block

Spring

Color for Spring - Green borders
CENTER:

    Block P1 - cut 1 - 6½" x 8½" of White A
    Block R1 - cut 1 - 8½" x 8½" of White A
    Block Q1 - cut 1 - 14½" x 20½" of White B

Use White leftovers for piecing:

    Block V1 - cut 4 - 2½" x 4½" White
    Block V1 - cut 1 - 3" x 3" White
    Block W1 - cut 4 - 2" x 8½" White
    Block W1 - cut 4 - 2" x 2" White
    Block U1 - cut 4 - 4" x 4" White

Colors:

    Block S1 - cut 1 - 2½" x 12½" Blue
    Block T1 - cut 1 - 2½" x 8½" Pink
    Block U1 - cut 4 - 4" x 4" Yellow
    Block V1 - cut 8 - 2½" x 2½" Blue
    Block V1 - cut 1 - 3" x 3" Blue
    Block W1 - cut 4 - 4½" x 2" Green
    Block W1 - cut 4 - 3" x 2" Green
    Block W1 - cut 4 - 2" x 2" Green

Q1 - Flower Garden Block

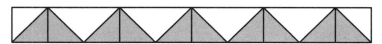

V1 - Flying Geese Block

R1 - Butterfly Block

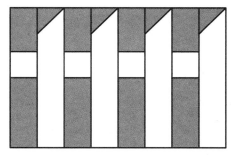

W1 - Fence Block

V1 - Flying Geese Block

TIP: See instructions for half-square triangle block on page 11.

V1 - FLYING GEESE BLOCKS

SMALL BLOCKS (A):
Use 1 - 3" x 3" White and 1 - 3" x 3" Blue.
Pair up two 3" x 3" squares together.
Draw a line from corner to corner on the diagonal.
Sew a seam ¼" on each side of the diagonal line.
Cut apart on the diagonal line to make 2 squares.
Press.
Center and trim each half-square triangle block to
    2½" x 2½".
You made 2.

A   A

The pair of 3" x 3" squares will make 2 half-
square triangle blocks trimmed to 2½" x 2½".

LONG BLOCKS (B):
Use four 2½" x 4½" White strips and eight 2½" x 2½" Blue
    squares.
Align a 2½" x 2½" Blue square on the left corner of a White
    strip.
Draw a line from corner to corner on the diagonal.
Sew on the diagonal line.
Fold the Blue back and press.
Trim off excess fabric underneath.
Make 4.

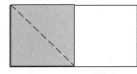 

Blue   White

Line up another 2½" x 2½" Blue square on the right corner.
Draw a line from corner to corner on the diagonal.
Sew on the diagonal line.
Press.
Fold the Blue back and press.
Trim off excess fabric underneath.
Make 4.

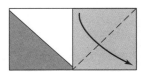 

Sew an A Block, 4 B Blocks, and an A Block together. Press.

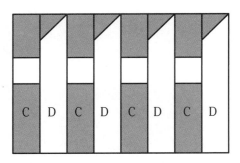

W1 - Fence Block

W1 - FENCE BLOCK

FENCE COLUMNS (D):
Use four 2" x 8½" White and four 2" x 2" Green.
Align a 2" x 2" Green on the top edge of a White strip.
Draw a line from corner to corner on the diagonal.
Sew on the diagonal line.
Fold the Green back and press.
Trim off excess fabric underneath.
Make 4.

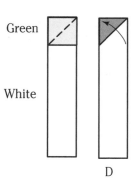

Green

White

D

BACKGROUND AND WHITE COLUMNS (C):
Use four 2" x 4½" Green,
    four 2" x 2½" White and
    four 2" x 3" Green.
Sew a column together -
    2" x 2½" Green - 2" x 2" White - 2" x 4½" Green.
Press.
Make 4.

C

ASSEMBLE FENCE COLUMNS:
Sew columns C and D together side by side to
    complete the fence.

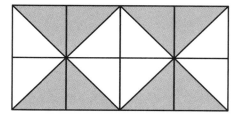

U1 - Hourglass Block

TIP: See instructions for half-square triangle block
     on page 11.

U1 - HOURGLASS BLOCKS:
    Use four 4" x 4" White and four 4" x 4" Yellow.
    Pair up two 4" x 4" color squares together.
    Draw a line from corner to corner on the diagonal.
    Sew a seam ¼" on each side of the diagonal line.
    Cut apart on the diagonal line to make 2 squares.
    Press.
    Center and trim each half-square triangle block to
        3½" x 3½".
    Make 4.

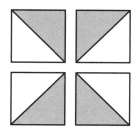

Position 4 blocks into a square, note the position.
Sew the 4 blocks together. Press.
Trim each Hourglass block to 6½" x 6½".
Make 2.
Sew the 2 Hourglass blocks together to make
    a block 6½" x 12½".

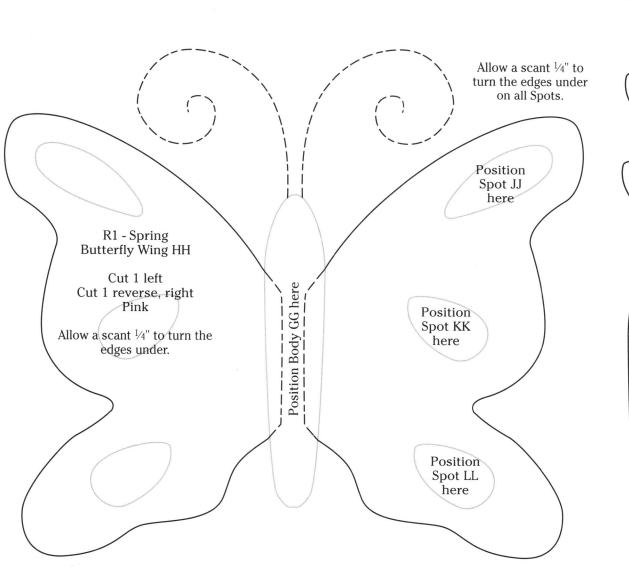

Allow a scant ¼" to
turn the edges under
on all Spots.

Spot JJ
Cut 2
Blue

Spot KK
Cut 2
Blue

Spot LL
Cut 2
Blue

Position
Spot JJ
here

Position
Spot KK
here

Position
Spot LL
here

R1 - Spring
Butterfly Wing HH

Cut 1 left
Cut 1 reverse, right
Pink

Allow a scant ¼" to turn the
edges under.

Position Body GG here

R1 - Spring - Butterfly Body GG - Cut 1 Blue
Allow a scant ¼" to turn the edges under.

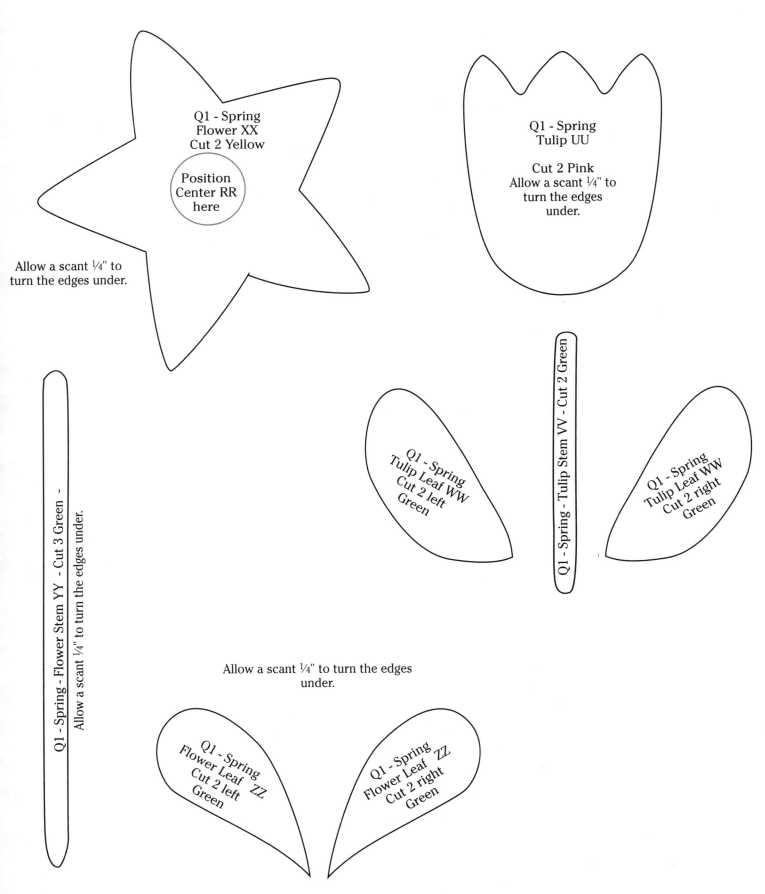

Q1 - Spring
Flower XX
Cut 2 Yellow

Position
Center RR
here

Q1 - Spring
Tulip UU

Cut 2 Pink
Allow a scant ¼" to
turn the edges
under.

Allow a scant ¼" to
turn the edges under.

Q1 - Spring - Flower Stem YY - Cut 3 Green -
Allow a scant ¼" to turn the edges under.

Q1 - Spring - Tulip Stem VV - Cut 2 Green

Q1 - Spring
Tulip Leaf WW
Cut 2 left
Green

Q1 - Spring
Tulip Leaf WW
Cut 2 right
Green

Allow a scant ¼" to turn the edges
under.

Q1 - Spring
Flower Leaf ZZ
Cut 2 left
Green

Q1 - Spring
Flower Leaf ZZ
Cut 2 right
Green

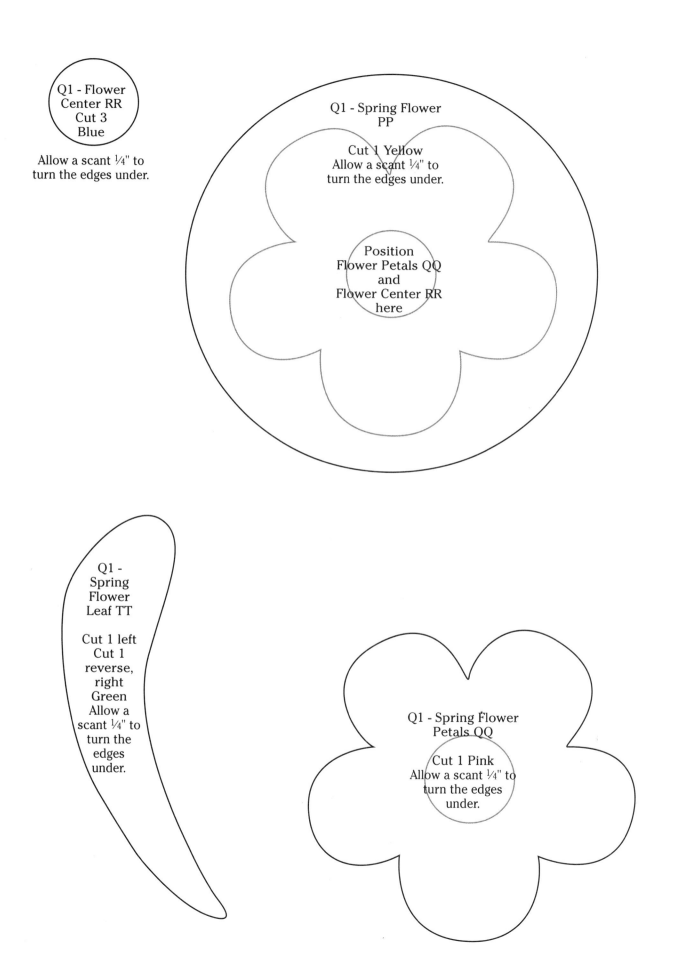

Q1 - Flower
Center RR
Cut 3
Blue

Allow a scant ¼" to
turn the edges under.

Q1 - Spring Flower
PP

Cut 1 Yellow
Allow a scant ¼" to
turn the edges under.

Position
Flower Petals QQ
and
Flower Center RR
here

Q1 - Spring Flower Stem SS - Cut 1 Green - Allow a scant ¼" to turn the edges under.

Q1 -
Spring
Flower
Leaf TT

Cut 1 left
Cut 1
reverse,
right
Green
Allow a
scant ¼" to
turn the
edges
under.

Q1 - Spring Flower
Petals QQ

Cut 1 Pink
Allow a scant ¼" to
turn the edges
under.

P1 - Spring
Bird Wing NN-2

Cut 1 Blue

Allow a scant ¼" to
turn the edges under.

P1 - Spring
Bird Wing NN

Cut 1 Pink
Allow a scant ¼" to turn
the edges under.

Position
Bird Wings
NN and NN-2
here

P1 - Spring
Bird Beak OO

Cut a 1½" square. Fold
it three times to form a
beak shape. Press each
fold. Tuck the raw edges
under the bird body.

P1 - Spring
Bird Body MM

Cut 1 Blue
Allow a scant ¼" to turn the
edges under.

ASSEMBLE BLOCKS:
Assemble the 8 blocks as shown on pages 24 and 25.

APPLIQUE THE DESIGN BLOCKS - P1, Q1 and R1:
Cut out the designs.
Applique the pieces in the method of your choice, see page 10.
Embroider the butterfly antennae and the bird eye with
    Tan pearl cotton (or 6-ply floss) and a #22 Chenille needle.

1 corner square - 1 block - 1 strip - 1 block - 1 square

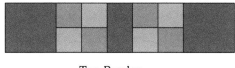

Top Border

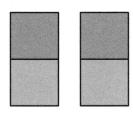

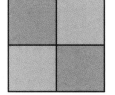

4-Patch Checkerboard

BORDER - CHECKERBOARD BLOCKS:
Small Quilt:
    Cut 24 - 4½" x 9" strips.
    Sort the colors into pairs of 2 strips.
    Sew strips together side by side to make a piece 8½" x 9".
    Cut into strips 4½" x 8½".
    Sort the colors again into pairs of 2 strips
    Sew strips together side by side to make a 4-Patch
        checkerboard.
    Make 12.

Single 4 Seasons Quilt: Make six 4-Patch blocks (see page 34).

FOR SMALL QUILT BORDER
Each Border block will measure 8" x 8" finished.

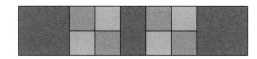

Bottom Border

Top and Bottom Borders:

Sew the following:
    1 corner square - 1 block - 1 strip - 1 block - 1 square
        together for the top and bottom borders. Press.

    Center Strips for Top and Bottom Borders:
        From leftover colors cut 2 strips 4½" x 8½".

    Corner Squares:
        Cut 4 squares - 8½" x 8½."

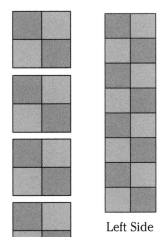

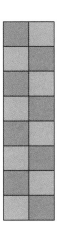

Left Side   Right Side

Four 4-Patch

Position blocks around the center for desired color placement.
Side Borders:
    Sew 4 blocks together for the side rows.
    Make 2. Press.

SMALL QUILT BORDER
    Sew side borders to the quilt center.
    Sew top and bottom borders to the quilt. Press.

BINDING:
    Cut strips 2½" wide.
    Sew together end to end to equal 178".
    See Binding Instructions on page 11.

OR FOR LARGE QUILT and BORDER - see pages 32 - 34.

Lap Quilt - Variation

FINISHED SIZE: 46" x 74"
Refer to page 5. Make blocks A1, B1, C1, and D1.
Refer to page 7. Make 8 Log Cabin blocks.
Refer to page 13. Make blocks M1, O1, and N1.
Refer to page 16. Make 8 half-square triangle blocks.
Assemble as shown. Press.

Additional Yardage:
  ½ yard for border #1
  2 yards for border #2 and binding
  2½ yards for backing

Inner Border #1:
Cut 1½" strips by the width of fabric.
Sew strips together end to end.
  Cut 2 strips 1½" x 64½" for sides.
  Cut 2 strips 1½" x 38½" for top and bottom.
  Sew side borders to the quilt. Press.
  Sew top and bottom borders to the quilt.
  Press.

Outer Border #2:
Cut strips 4½" wide parallel to the selvage
 to eliminate piecing.
  Cut 2 strips 4½" x 66½" for sides.
  Cut 2 strips 4½" x 46½" for top and bottom.
  Sew side borders to the quilt. Press.
  Sew top and bottom borders. Press.

FINISHING:
Quilting:
  See Basic Instructions on pages 9 - 11.
Binding:
  Cut strips 2½" wide.
  Sew together end to end to equal 250". Sew to quilt.

Large Lap Quilt - Variation

FINISHED SIZE: 52" x 76"
Refer to page 5. Make blocks A1, B1, C1, and D1.
Refer to page 13. Make blocks M1, O1, and N1.
Refer to page 19. Make blocks E1, F1, G1, H1, I1, J1, K1, and L1.
Refer to page 25. Make blocks P1, Q1, R1, S1, T1, U1, V1, and W1.
Assemble as shown. Press.

Additional Yardage:
  ½ yard for border #1
  2 yards for border #2 and binding
  3 yards for backing

Inner Border #1:
Cut 2½" strips by the width of fabric.
Sew strips together end to end.
  Cut 2 strips 2½" x 64½" for sides.
  Cut 2 strips 2½" x 44½" for top and bottom.
  Sew side borders. Press. Sew top and bottom borders. Press.

Outer Border #2:
Cut strips 4½" wide parallel to the selvage to eliminate piecing.
  Cut 2 strips 4½" x 68½" for sides.
  Cut 2 strips 4½" x 52½" for top and bottom.
  Sew side borders. Press. Sew top and bottom borders. Press.

FINISHING:
Quilting: See Basic Instructions on pages 9 - 11.
Binding: Cut strips 2½" wide.
  Sew together end to end to equal 266". Sew to quilt.

Pieced Border #1:
Repeat the Pieced Border #1 from the
   Single quilt on page 34.

Pieced Border #2:
Left Side Border:
Sew 5 Log Cabins and 5 Half-
   square triangles. Press.

Right Side Border:
Sew a set of 20 Piano Keys to
   5 checkerboards. Press.
Top Border:
Sew a Corner square-Log Cabin-
   2 strips-2 Log Cabins-a 14 Piano
   Key strip-Corner square. Press.
Bottom Border:
Sew a Corner square-2 Half-square
   triangles-Light strip-Half-square
   triangle-2 Checkerboards-Dark
   strip-Checkerboard-Corner square.
Sew side borders to the quilt.
   Press.
Sew top and bottom borders to the
   quilt. Press.

Inner Border #3:
Cut 2½" strips by the width of fabric.
Sew strips together end to end.
   Cut 2 strips 2½" x 96½" for sides.
   Cut 2 strips 2½" x 76½" for top
      and bottom.
Sew side borders to the quilt. Press.
Sew top and bottom borders to the
   quilt. Press.

Outer Border #4:
Cut strips 6½" wide parallel to the
      selvage to eliminate piecing.
   Cut 2 strips 6½" x 100½" for sides.
   Cut 2 strips 6½" x 88½" for top
      and bottom.
Sew side borders to the quilt. Press.
Sew top and bottom borders to the
   quilt. Press.

FINISHING:
Quilting:
See Basic Instructions on pages 9 - 11.

Binding:
Cut strips 2½" wide.
Sew together end to end to equal 410".
See Binding Instructions on page 11.

Queen Quilt – Variation

FINISHED SIZE: 88" x 112"
Construct the quilt center following the instructions for the Single Bed Quilt.
Refer to pages 7-8. Make 14 Log Cabin blocks, two 2-strip Center Strips, and 8 Corner Squares.
Refer to page 16. Make 14 half-square triangle blocks. Cut 2 Light strips 4½" x 8½".
Refer to page 23. Make 1 set of 10, 1 set of 14, 1 set of 16 and 1 set of 20 piano keys.
Refer to page 31. Make fourteen 4-patch checkerboard blocks. Cut 2 Dark strips 4½" x 8½".

Additional Yardage:
   ¾ yard for border #3
   3 yards for border #4 and binding
   7½ yards for backing

Single Bed Quilt – Variation

FINISHED SIZE: 72" x 96"

Construct the quilt center following the instructions for the Large Lap Quilt (page 32).

Refer to pages 7-8. Make 6 Log Cabin blocks, a 2-strip Center Strip, and 4 Corner Squares.

Refer to page 16. Make 6 half-square triangle blocks. Cut 1 Light strip 4½" x 8½".

Refer to page 23. Make 1 set of 16 and 1 set of 10 piano keys.

Refer to page 31. Make six 4-patch checkerboard blocks.

Cut 1 Dark strip 4½" x 8½".

Additional Yardage:
¾ yard for border #2
2½ yards for border #3 and binding
4 yards for backing

Pieced Border #1:
Left Side Border:
Sew 4 Log Cabins and 4 Half-square triangles. Press.

Right Side Border:
Sew the 16 Piano Key strip to 4 checkerboards. Press.

Top Border:
Sew a Corner square-Log Cabin-2 strips-Log Cabin-10 Piano Key strip-Corner square. Press.

Bottom Border:
Sew a Corner square-Half-square triangle-Light strip-Half-square triangle-Checkerboard-Dark strip-Checkerboard-Corner square.
Sew side borders to the quilt. Press.
Sew top and bottom borders to the quilt. Press.

Inner Border #2:
Cut 2½" strips.
Sew strips together end to end.
Cut 2 strips 2½" x 80½" for sides.
Cut 2 strips 2½" x 60½" for top and bottom.
Sew side borders to the quilt. Press.
Sew top and bottom borders to the quilt. Press.

Outer Border #3:
Cut strips 6½" wide parallel to the selvage to eliminate piecing.
Cut 2 strips 6½" x 84½" for sides.
Cut 2 strips 6½" x 72½" for top and bottom.
Sew side borders to the quilt. Press.
Sew top and bottom borders to the quilt. Press.

FINISHING:
Quilting:
See Basic Instructions on pages 9 - 11.
Binding:
Cut strips 2½" wide.
Sew together end to end to equal 346".
See Binding Instructions on page 11.

Basic Instructions for Cutting, Sewing, Layering, Quilting and Binding are on pages 9 - 11.

TIPS: As a Guide for Yardage:
Each ¼ yard or a 'Fat Quarter' equals 3 strips.
A pre-cut 'Jelly Roll' strip is 2½" x 44".
Cut 'Fat Quarter' and yardage strips to 2½" x 22".

Yardage is given for using either 'Jelly Roll' strips or fabric yardage.

Supplier - Most quilt and fabric stores carry an excellent assortment of supplies. If you need something special, ask your local store to contact the following companies.

FABRICS, 'JELLY ROLLS', 'FAT QUARTERS'
Moda and United Notions, Dallas, TX, 972-484-8901

QUILTER
Julie Lawson, 817-428-5929

MANY THANKS to my staff for their cheerful help and wonderful ideas!
Kathy Mason • Patty Williams • Janet Long • David & Donna Thomason
Donna Kinsey for skillfully and patiently editing the instructions in this book